Waving at Trains

John Dickson

ThornTree Press, inc.

Acknowledgement is given to the following for the first publication of some of these poems: American Scholar, Blue Unicorn, Circus Maximus, Epos, Harper's, Images, Jean's Journal, Kansas Quarterly, Midway Review, Negative Capability, Nit & Wit, Overtures, Passages North, Poet & Critic, Pulpsmith, Rhino, Salome, Scarab, Southern Poetry Review, Spoon River Quarterly, Stone Country. "Feeding the Neighbor's Cat," "Quiet Zone," "Fugue," and "A Tale of Two Cities" permission of Poetry. "Wheat" and "Aragon Ballroom" permission of Tri-Quarterly.

By the same author: Victoria Hotel (Chicago Review Press, 1979)

Cover design Laura M. Doyle
Logo design by Laura M. Doyle
Photography by Vicki Grayland
Typography by Patricia Wilson Barnes
Layout by Martin Bartels

Special thanks to David Simonson, editor and publisher, Pioneer Press, and to John Daiberl

ISBN (Clothbound) 0-939395-06-1
ISBN (Paperback) 0-939395-07-X
Library of Congress Catalog Number: 86-050928

Published in 1986 by
Thorntree Press, Inc.
547 Hawthorn Lane
Winnetka, Ill. 60093

Contents

MATERNITY WARD

Behold the enemy,
dropping into life like petals on water,
whisked from fluid to substance to blanket
to numbered basket in the sterile room
screaming, "Take this cup from me!"
Shielded from sunlight.
Weaned from the dark.

And oh, the proud relatives,
noticing in them the father's eye
the mother's nose, the uncle's jaw
but failing to detect the tendency
to see and take.

All of them have built-in mechanisms
set to release in them the various means
of conquering and owning --
by logic, love or force --
with all the emotional detachment
of the lion or the shark.

They will discover sex and mind and moon,
lay claim to the world and usurp my place --
first wait on my table, then own it
deliver my paper, then write it
drive my train, love me, marry me, tax me.
Mug me.
Sweep me off the earth
back to the land they have come from.

Now, like fanatics shouting in the streets
their voices penetrate the sound-proof glass:
"We will own you! We will bury you!"
But one smiles at me. At me!
That makes up for everything.

SWEET SHOP

The first two Greeks of my life
end-products of ancient philosophers
worried at the window of their Sweet Shop
moustached and quiet except for
occasional iron words bolted together.
The clock on the murky wall
chopped off minutes, one by one.

Sometimes I spent a penny there.
Sometimes I spent a nickel.
Once I bought my lunch --
the air filmy with burgers and fries
rich with coffee and catsup and fruit
sweet with malt and caramel
pineapple sodas
chocolate and walnut and mint.
When I bought a piece of candy
the Greeks would never smile.

Usually the Sweet Shop was empty.
Sometimes a man no one knew,
deep eyes with no reflection,
sat in one of the dark booths
grinding his jaws. . .crunching his meal.
Sometimes at one of the marble-topped tables
a large-hatted woman in loose clothes
sat alone talking and swallowing
mingling her words with her ice cream,
and always the tragic Greeks --
hillsides of goats. . .valleys of grapes. . .
washing the glasses
wiping the marble
dying in the shadow of their food.

There were sounds of a family somewhere in back
maybe thin-legged olive-eyed children
maybe a stringy woman
limping about with her spirit broken
bewildered by our flat country
longing for some particular hill.

I wish they had played Greek music
or told me of their crossing the ocean
or of islands in the Aegean Sea.
All I knew of them was school-book Ulysses
and the Trojan War
and Diogenes in his tub.

THE FAMILY

The family in its stone walls
between lamp black and dog howl
between the last five stars and dawn.
The father, his eye of a trout,
lies between the cloister of the womb
and his last aloneness
lies in his floating bed and never sleeps.
The daughter, her eye of the bird
her eye of the young doe
lies between heartbreak and madness
studying the moon in its cool round.
The mother lights fires in the kitchen
lights fires in her eyes
her mind of flowered wallpaper
her memories a wilted corsage
her hope the flower of the moon.

The family at its walnut table --
crystal and linen and glistening silver.
The clock on the wall destroying time.
Portraits straining to leave their frames,
to abdicate the family.
The father folding his bones neatly in his chair
praying, Dominus Vobiscum
holding his fork like a shovel.
The daughter with porcelain skin
her voice like sun slanting through the window
her fingers like wings as she holds her cup.
The mother an aging Cinderella
lost in a forest of long-ago faces
her voice the whisper of Spanish moss
one foot deformed by its glass slipper.

The family in its walled yard
in its hanging gardens
in its white gazebo watching the sunset
the sky's fire turning to dust.
The father's face an iron gate
his mind somewhere else.
The daughter waiting for fireflies
waiting for comets
for the tip of the moon in its act of rising
for invading soldiers to carry her off.
The mother with her collapsed smile
veils and shawls and facial hair.
Tightening her web
with memories of times past.
Binding the three of them together,
lampreys clinging to her words.

The family sealed in its stone walls
in its large rooms
waiting for yesterday.

THE MAID

Margaret working in the kitchen
mixing raisins in the butter
stirring flour in the eggs.
Thinks of home in Indiana --
corn and oats and cottonwood.

Speaks of barns and cows and chickens,
wagons on the gravel road
fishing in the muddy river
swimming in the pond.

Margaret in her room at night.
Iron bed and maple dresser
pictures of her brother's family
homesick, studying the ceiling.
Ample hips that yearn for children.
Dark hair underneath her arms.

Thursdays off and part of Sunday
walking with the grocer's clerk,
driving with the quiet druggist
Indiana in her eyes.
Then one Monday, humming. . .singing. . .
scrubbing floors and washing windows
painting chairs and mending curtains.
Wednesday, bakes my favorite cake,
packs her things and goes back home.

FEEDING THE NEIGHBOR'S CAT

Like an accomplished thief
I slip the key in the lock
and enter the house of the lone cat.
There is a chill in the stale rooms
a quiet of floor creak and faucet drip.

I begin the game we play
searching with mock concern and finally find her
hiding in the jungle by the window
or watching from behind the fireplace screen.
As soon as I discover her the game is ended
and she makes sounds like a distant motor boat
strains her cat muscles stretching
or engages me in light conversation.

There is something about this cat --
the eyes. . .the way they shine.
I knew a girl who had such eyes --
Felicia What's-her-name. . .lost track of years ago
but now she is this cat completely.

Sometimes we race through the rambling house
clattering our echoes through the rooms.
If I catch her I flip her over
toss her high in the air
strip her of all her regality.
Sometimes she'll claw or bite and then apologize
growing quiet and sit by me,
looking up with her Felicia eyes.
She knows when I'm about to leave
and disappears, not one to show her feelings.

Sometimes in the afternoon or late at night
I walk past and look at the old house
aware that she's in there waiting
watching from each of its dozen windows.
If only she weren't so unrealistic --
her age times seven makes her barely twelve
and besides, she's locked up in a cat.

DISPOSSESSED

The time we were evicted
the day we were evicted --
something to do with mortgages and money --
all of us loading the things in a rented truck
Dad throwing away, throwing away
with a strange frenzy
Mother salvaging and carefully wrapping
my sister with her own things
unhappy in her own way
and me long since packed
working and furious, removing
pictures and unknown relatives from the walls
and carrying them out to the truck.
Dust older than I streaming out the window
old wooden chairs worn smoooth
by generations of exhausted rumps
insects wriggling from the closets
lint balls and mouse hair
long lost pennies and papers under the rugs.

The sun that had risen with such fire and flair
had dwindled down to a pale coin.
This side of noon I sat in the truck to wait,
watching the house change from wood to stone
reliving days I had forgotten
conjuring foggy memories --
fog dog barking from the porch
fog mother calling from the window.
I would carry this house on my shoulders forever
wear it around my neck
maybe now and then dissolve the world with it
as you dissolve a vampire by holding up a cross.

Finally we drove away
the trees pulling at me
the flowers pulling at me
the attic of my solitude
the sight of Loretta from across the street. . .
everything pulling at me.
But still we drove away.

Years of remembering the day
but forgetting the house.
Was there a pantry between the kitchen and the hall?
Was there a window by the stairs?
I remember fog in the mornings
sun in the afternoons
and the tree I used to climb.
But the house doesn't matter anymore.
I've passed it several times lately
without bothering to look.

THE ARAGON BALLROOM

I could hear the music as I waited to be born --
Wayne King the Waltz King and his golden sax
rolling across the roofs and through the alleys
and into our windows down the street
making my feet move, making me wonder
what sort of planet I'd come to, anyway.
And later as I crawled through Persian patterns of the rugs
and later still as I memorized my night paths
behind the stores and through the shadowy streets,
clarinets and trumpets heralded my way.

But in less time than you'd think I learned that place --
by day how it slept through roars of the passing 'L's,
through sooty pigeons cooing at the windows,
and by night how it turned to plaster Spain inside --
gold statues of caballeros and their senoritas
and the thick red carpet stretching from the ticket taker
into the illusion paradise of yellow balconies
with vines and bright balloons and tiled roofs
that scraped the Spanish sky of faint electric stars.

And all the Lorettas and Teresas, Margies and Maries
half floosie, half madonna in their first high heels,
the smell of soap, the smell of sharp cologne,
drawn there on those nights to come alive
with some Sam or Tony, Mario or Fred,
lanky, muscle-bound, or Mr. Five-by-Five
but necessarily capable of serious dancing --
either to the organ shuddering through the building
or to a wispy saxophone, snare drum and brushes
for drifting and weaving around the floor.

And off in the haze beyond the dancers
or up in the shadows of the balcony
the crewcuts and greasers busy as scheming roosters,
surveying the crop, considering anything fair game --
girls who lived for their mothers
or those with whom no one would dance.
Girls still homesick for small town families

or those who could barely look up from their shyness
lost in their loneliness of make-up and corsage,
blaming themselves for even being there.

And always on the fire escape of summer nights,
the bright dress and dark suit of quiet intermission.
And always at the tables of the soft drink stand
those long conversations of serious intent.
And always the ultimate weddings of relatives and wine
held in the Halls for All Occasions,
always the painted wedding photographs
of responsible grooms and basic brides --
eyes blue, lips red, and cheeks unnatural pink.

But now only the whisper of those lives
rushes through the empty building
with echoes of Old Black Magic and Small Hotel,
Take the A-Train, Adios, and Blue Room.
And all those nights, as though imbedded in amber,
kept safe or worn as charms,
through hospitals or wars or blahs
as a reminder of those nights in Spain
or just of partners who could really dance.

DOCTOR QUINN

Mouths come to him
with their snaggleteeth and molars
and malocclusions of the lower jaw,
quiet more often than not
though sometimes screaming.
And he stands there picking away. . .drilling away. . .
healing them
dreaming of teeth he's known before --
concrete teeth of men with castiron hands
teeth like knives for tearing or ripping
or woebegotten teeth as soft as cheese
that wince and turn away --
teeth that could gnaw down trees
or weak teeth in the final quadrant of their years --
all with last night's dinner turned to rot.

He will say, I've got just the girl for you --
firm jaw and even bite.
Call this number. . .go to this address
and see the work I've done. . .
gingival margins. . .anatomy of the tooth.
And all the while he stands there
drilling decay or scraping plaque.

Frequently a nightmare comes to him
high in the murk above his bed
or in the shadows of the street
or while he dozes on a crowded bus,
when the infinite face-slits come alive
and yawn into chasms of red satin mouths
pink plastic mouths
shrewish mouths or sensual mouths
or mouths of sour beer or furry breath,
each rimmed by gleaming parapets of teeth
to guard a quivering, defiant tongue.

He will say, This girl has an oval face. . .
well balanced. . .really beautiful. . .
lives on a street where elm trees arch across.
Notice the fine alignment of her jaw
and the close-matched color of her upper plate.
Mention my name. . .she'll understand.
Here -- just call this number.

FACES

The cows all huddling together like cows,
the one lone tree standing out in the field
with no one to talk to,
and me waving at trains --
sometimes in the morning,
sometimes in the afternoon --
standing down by the fence. . .by the creek. . .
by the edge of the farm, waving
just to become a part of the world.
And all those constantly serious faces
hypnotized by the barley and oats
or the fluttering by of utility poles,
like faces painted on the windows
of trains that roared by like screaming birds --
a woman with shiny sequined brows
a Scheherazady girl who dreamed at me
a man who wore an Assyrian beard --
their blank expressions with me all these years,
those people who never waved back.

I see faces like theirs here and there
in elevators or on the street
and greet them as I did back then --
Scheherazade who is usually alone,
who gives off the sudden scent of fear
as though I carried a folding bed,
who'd gladly tell me stories for a thousand nights
if only I'd spare her life.
Or someome like the woman with sequined brows
who either turns the place blue with police
or instantly blindfolds my casual "hello"
and has it summarily shot.
Even the man with the Assyrian beard,
all briefcase and business and balance sheets
who waves his hand like a magic wand
and makes me disappear.

RITES OF PRINTEMPS

> Awake! For morning in the bowl of night
> has flung the stone that puts the stars to flight.
> -- the Rubaiyat

It's April, and I'm slowly turning green.
It's spring! It's here, and those who have survived
the winter of steam heat chained to their desks,
shoes nailed to the floor, seek out the sun
and dance their dance to unaccompanied flute
while aging bachelor girls sway through the streets,
their winter clothes sloughed off like last year's skin
and cause several minor traffic jams
with their blazing girdles and brassieres
as chlorophyll keeps rising in my veins.

Monarchs and other future butterflies
rattle in their cocoons, and so far
several Greeks from Harrison and Halsted
have abducted rather heavy brides,
and from the platforms of their loading docks
the boys of forehead horns and cloven hoof
yell springtime ritual propositions
to girls as thin as trees at timberline
who tap their pizzicato down the street,
filling out before your very eyes.
O spring. . .O whistling woman. . .O crowing hen --
the earth has swung to April once again.

OPEN HOUSE

We are strapped to our chairs by acceptable manners
while tedious words wait in line to be said.
Conversations crawl over me
nipping sharply like hungry mice.

Flowers feed on the sun through the window,
the guitar on the floor recalls old songs
and the candles yearn for flames to consume them.

My ship lies awash in an ocean of words.
As I leave, shaking hands, its transmitter cries,
"May Day! May Day! I'm sinking fast!"
but you sit with your antenna down
pleasantly smiling.

THE NIGHT THE DORFMANS MET

There were ten of us in the apartment that night,
maybe twelve -- all sitting around with drinks
and little fish-and-cheesy things --
Carla exhausted by this Joseph Dorfman person
stumbling over his tongue through broken sentences
and trailing conversations.

But what would she have him do?
. . .touch her as he felt like doing?
. . .carve their initials on the furniture?
. . .tell all these strangers this was it at last?
Instead, he sat there like a wall clock
grinding his present into the past,
memorizing her long green eyes,
studying how a few lines of her face
manipulated all her smiles and ponderings
as she spoke to him of unimportant things,
little tortures of What did he do? What did he think?
he studying the carved legs of the piano.

And the piano just standing there
silent as he was, waiting to be touched,
to be brought to life, its taut wires quivering,
humming faint harmonies of occasional
deep voices or explosions of laughter.
Finally Carla giving up and moving across the room
leaving him suddenly desperate,
suddenly flinging himself at the piano,
pounding it, whipping it like a horse
to carry them away to arpeggios of mountain streams
with torrents of tumbling double chords.

Then pianissimos of things he hadn't said to her
and cyclones of chromatics that shook the room,
a prelude to things he'd spend forever saying --
all sounds of Joseph Dorfman speaking.

THE STEEPLE

I drive down winding roads with Amy
and stop at my discarded church,
its bell cracked and its clapper gone.
We creak through the door to the vaulted room,
the pulpit there, but no seats.
Only a litter of hymnals and beer cans
and little heaps of unanswered prayers.
Only gullies worn on the floor
by families and families of knees.

We open the door to the dark stairs,
feel each step to the endless climb
to the tower of the quiet bell
and look out across the willow tops,
climb to the wind-whish up the steeple loft
and look out across the sun-washed fields.

Around us initials and dates of love
are carved on the loft ledge --
hearts and arrows and "Ruth" and "Sam."
Below us the weathered gravestones
sleep in their churchyard.
Birds fly between the cherry trees like thoughts
and off in their field the cows
are all facing Mecca.

I think, Amy. . .Amy. . .now is the time,
now before we're as old as the church
as old as these rafters, old as the bell,
before we spin off to the starry path
or lose ourselves in the night sounds.

But there are no wires between us,
no hand-touch nor eye-talk
and our names don't belong on the rafters.
She says, It's quite a long way to the ground.
I say, This must be a very old church.
Below us the cherry trees are in blossom
and the willows flow along their rivers

off to the forest on the horizon.
Above us hangs the corroded bell,
no longer able to say what it feels.

We linger up there for a long time
to delay going back down the dark stairs.

19

ERASING THE TASTE OF LOVE TURNED SOUR
BY UNLIVING IT BACK TO A POINT
PRECEDING ITS INCEPTION

It ended with a bonfire late at night,
the flames of all her letters I had saved
confirming the orange hate behind my eyes
and lighting up the back yard where I stood,
the bushes around me dancing black and yellow.

After dinner, as the sun rose in the west,
I ran storming back to afternoon
and there on the path along the river
the two of us held our verbal duel,
her rage as bright as her burning letters,
our poison-tipped words aimed purposely to kill
and fired, each reserving our regrets for later on.
Until we noticed the park and its trees
and the boats in the river, walked off hand in hand,
sat in a restaurant with our birds-nest soup,
then kissed hello and went our separate ways.

And after that, those getting unacquainted times,
each day tinged with its own delicate madness
of wanting to be together, each day a cameo
framed by whispers of guitar or muted trumpet
and, as though the days were not enough,
each was followed by a letter praising it,
letters I would read and read
and add to the dwindling packet I was saving.

And then that first day, fresher than the rest,
sitting together at the picnic table,
me studying the smile lines of her face
the leafy shadows of her hair -- each of us
ignoring shouts of burlap races and volley ball
around us until we finally met
just as afternoon merged into morning.

Since then there's nothing I recall;
each day has been the same old tooth.
Maybe I've passed her on the street
or sat beside her in a coffee shop
asking for the sugar or the cream
but since we've never met, I'll never know.

21

THE LEGEND

It is a legend saved and savored
by shadows under the eaves,
branches that scrape the worn roof
and the whishing whispers of the knee-high lawn.

Told and retold in the passing cars
how a lifetime ago in that paint-chipped house
while the bridesmaids stood in the front hall
waiting to catch the bride's bouquet
crying their laughs and flinging their rice,
silk in their smiles and moon in their lace,
the groom slumped slowly to the floor.

Told how the clocks stopped,
how the flowers turned dry
and the white lace yellowed,
how the left-over wedding cake turned to stone
and the car stood empty in the drive --
its fenders and running boards turned to rust,
its tires dead and its spirit flown.

And the bride.
And her ring.
And her crumpled face and her crippled dress
wandering through years of not belonging,
living in her cluttered rooms
of peaceful cats and deep-voiced hound
or living sort of a death on the porch
watching the unbelievable world
of beer cans and casual obscenities
tossed in her yard through summers of heat
and winters of snow on the sparrow's head.

Sometimes when the sun at evening
is flecks of amber in her eye
and shadows merge in the first stage of night
she will answer a voice that keeps hovering near
and shuffle inside
and close the door.

THE FIRST SUMMER WEEKEND

I say, Hey -- Where's Sam?
and get looks like where've I been?
Maybe sleeping twenty years in the hills
while my dog turns to bones and a skull
and my gun a sprinkle of rust.

Of course the world is still here
and we're all lying on the sand again
on the stretch of beach near the ribbon grass
and like every other summer
the sun burns away our memories of winter
and young girls run through the surf
to remind us of living.

But there's this emptiness where Sam should be,
this feeling of something I left unsaid,
something I always wanted to tell him
all those years.
Now and then the shadow of a cloud
confirms his absence.

The crash of the waves on the rocks is the same
and the trees on the bluff still touch the sky,
but this time Sam is missing
and suddenly the beach seems empty.
Oh Death -- what a stupid ass you are.

AH, MCNEALY

Nipped in the bud in the dead of winter,
whisked from his crysallis oxygen tent
to a patch of ice in Memorial Park
behind the Housing Authority complex.
Had to chip out a spot for him
in the frozen clay --
he with his life-long hunger for sunshine
and his undying contempt for death.
And so abysmally cold every winter
even in thermal underwear.

But there's so much death been going around
that eulogies are out of date,
the whimpering dogs are never still
and old friends are constantly bowing their heads.
But McNealy --
I hate death more than ever now
for laying him low in such a sneaky way.
McNealy, all his life chained to that ponderous face,
sauntering along with his World's Fair cane
like he owned the place.

But he lived a bit of life in his time,
prayed for some things he didn't need
and fell in sewers looking up at the stars.
And he said a few rather sensible things --
"Better to be puzzled by life than explain it away,"
or "More praying goes on in a brokerage office
than in church."
And when the grasshoppers were stirring
and water spiders raced over the ponds,
he would lie on his lumpy mattress
and strum his guitar for the girl down the hall,
stopping whenever the trains roared by.

When the pigeons fly off to think things over
and the worn-out crow pumps over the hill
I'll dismount the wild horse I've been riding so long

and stand beneath the sensitive trees
by his grave that urinalysis dogs keep sniffing
and pay my respects to McNealy.
But he, his head still growing hair
will care not a bit that I'm standing there
and I'll know what a waste of time it is
to dwell on the ghosts of yesterday --
go back down the road where the phone lines sag
and pay my respects to the living.

WHEAT

Sometimes I forget the wheat in me
just as I forget the lung swell or blood flow.
But to feel the cool amber of it
in the grain bin or the tempering tank
or as it roars to the conveyor from the truck
is enough to ripen the fields behind my eyes
where horizons are the only limit.

There is sun there, and cloud shadow, heat and rain
and wind whispering all the wheat names in my ears --
Manitoba and Kubanka
Red Durum and Dark Northern Spring
Kharkov, Michikov, and Flint --
all in those fields that were prairie once,
that were trees cleared and stumps burned
or rocks pried from the earth and carried off.

And there are grain men there
talking their price per bushel
talking chinch bugs, rust and blight,
betting their lives on sun and rain and frost,
always knowing the weather long before it comes.
Now and then they drink together
but each is lost in the future
lost in somewhere else,
waiting.

And all the while, slowly
slowly as green turns to yellow
as yellow turns to gold
the glumes grow loose on their spikes
until finally a day of clear sky or black clouds
when the grain crews with their huge machines
move like paddle wheels along the earth's rim
filling their wagonloads of wheat .

Sometimes I forget the wheat
just as I forget the Blue Star Mill
and how it was with us --
Al with grain dust part of his lungs and hair,
the two of us shouting over the roar --
the rolls stripping open the wheat
the constant banging of the shakers
the motors' whine and the drive belts' whacking.
But then on the way to work I see grain cars
being humped and shunted out in Markham Yards
and it all comes back to life again.

FLOOD STAGE

The river rises
filling the gopher holes
chasing insects up the trees
engulfing the grey oak and the birch
and the train struggling through the valley
drowning the drivers waiting for the lights to change
as it roars down the street.

The Friday afternoon drinkers
sit in the River's Edge Tavern
snails on their faces
moss in their hair
floating an inch or two over their bar stools
studying their bilgy beer.

And there is a sediment of tables and chairs
where the streets were
wagons and cows and pencils
bewildered ducks and doomed rats
epic poems with distended bellies
percussion and woodwinds and brass

and a house floating downstream
sinking slowly as water pours through its keyhole —
letters under the floorboards
and a clock unwinding on the wall.
The face of a catfish is at the window
watching mice in the mud turn to fossil.

Surely, when the waters subside,
rushes and swamp grass will grow in the light
and mosquitoes heavy with blood
will rule the persistent damp.
The sun will be fogged forever
with spores of mushroom and mold
and salamanders and toads shall inherit the earth
because Dry will have become a lost word.
Dry will never happen.

DROUTH

The sun with its ancient fire
traces a fever chart to noon
baking pavements of fields
and memories of ponds.

Dry soil sifts through the fingers.
Now and then a cloud of no promise
marks the cracked earth
like the shadow of some carrion bird.

The sun moves on to horizons of cities
burning the streets and sizzling the roofs.
Our faces, pale from winter, turn up
to drink its heat.

But now in July the leaves are withering.
The grass has grown brown
and spilled beer dries quickly on the floor.

THE CONTRACT

It's really quite easy.
You go to a small table
deep in a tavern of blue lights
and wait.
Soon a man with a scar on his cheek
or a tattoo on his wrist
or a network of veins on his nose
will come to you
and you will count out the money
and he will ask if you're sure this is what you want
because after he leaves it will be too late.
You answer Yes, you are certain,
and then he leaves and it is too late
because you will never be able to find him again.

One day it will happen.
You won't know when.
Maybe the traffic jams will grow strangely quiet
or a stone bird up on the cornice of some old building
will begin to scream.
And you won't know how it happens.
There may be a darkness about his size
deep in the sluggish waters under the bridge
or maybe some lime will be sprinkled on the street
to eat up the stain of him.
Maybe one of his gloves will lie nearby.
But you will know
and you'll be free of him
since that's what you seem to want.

Maybe you'll forget him,
wear the mask of the bereaved wife
or remarry and put him out of your mind completely.
But maybe your days will turn to wood
and you'll walk cold in the shade
with his face floating in the air before you
and like obscene phone calls
your remorse will call out at unexpected times
and you'll recall only his fierce desire for you.

Still,
you've got to break some eggs to make an omelet.
Right, Baby?
Besides, it's easy. . .
you just go to the tavern of blue lights.

BLOOD DONATION

First the questionnaire.
Then clenching the fist
to bulge up the arm vein.
Soon this seeping away
out the needle and through the tube
like a maple tree being tapped
or a ruptured hour glass losing its time --
my life dripping into the small flask.

Is my shadow wilting?
Has my face dissolved?
There is a bird trapped inside my head
dashing itself against my eyes.
Do I still have a reflection in the mirror?
Darkness has come and there is no moon.

And the pulse -- I think it's dying.
My heart waits for the blood
that will never reach it.
Droplets of light in the empty veins
have turned my skin transparent.
Now my head is a white cloud
drifting along in its blue sea.

How gradually we die --
with each wrinkle
each extracted tooth
each love song outgrown and burned.
All my four-leaf clovers have lost a leaf.
Whoever receives my blood
will place his bets on the slow horse
spend hours recalling forgotten names
and dream hidden harbors and tall ships.

The nurse's face pours into my eyes.
Her voice sweeps over me like a wave.
She brings orange juice. . .
she brings life.

Time has run out in the parking meter
but I reach the office
only slightly late.

THE DASHING FIGURE

O where is Uncle George (Puff! Puff!)
Roaring over the house on business
hellbent for Bordeaux or Khartoum?
Rushing, of course,land waving,
flashing subliminal farewell smiles
as he fleetingly flits across the screen,
rushing to his uncertain future
like a man with his hair on fire.

In a droplet of water from the pond
are a hundred like Uncle George.
They are he, they are he,
fertilizing unremembered wives,
living their soon forgotten lives,
squirming compulsively through vague destinies
like multifaceted mindless men.

Something must save him or he will die
and the busy folks will have to pause
and quickly wave him away.
Perhaps some virulent fever
could burn off the subtle mist from his mind.
Or a blow on the head
could snip the wires of his torment.
Or a woman with time flowing through her
could trap him in her eye
and speak to him in words of sunlight and shadow.

I wave back at his pictures that hang in the hall,
the one of him waving
from the deck of the dwindling S.S. Maritza --
the one of him and his silk scarf waving
from the cockpit of the ancient plane.
Goodbye Uncle George!
Goodbye Uncle George!
And he smiles back waving. . .waving. . .waving. . .

THE TRAIN

Gophers scamper under the shed.
Birds huddle on their branch
feeling the tenseness of the tree
and the listening of its leaves.
Then, like a tremor of memory
a rumor of war
there is an awareness of the train --
all this before the walls speak
and the rooms sigh
and the rails hum beside the house.

A comment from the dishes
is the final warning.
And the ting of glasses on the shelf.
Then an explosion of pistons and wheels
rattles the windows, shudders the floor,
wracks the spine of the house
rupturing its timbers and joists,
ear drum and brain pan
and all our shouted words.

The room becomes sounds,
becomes a force ripping the air
flinging pans from the stove
and pictures from the walls.
Our faces are blurred with sound --
blood-churn and bone-throb.
Vines of plaster sift from the ceiling.
The room becomes a tunnel of echoes
a rumble of thunder
a memory of shock.

Even when we are away, far from the house,
the clocks in our blood run on time
and there is chaos when the train is due.
The floor shakes. . .the brain roars
even though where we are is quiet,
far from the rail pound and the wheel rush
and the train's lost call.

THE 7:09

My train on its thin tracks
moving past houses of wrinkled roofs
past the girl on her porch,
my train caught in her eye.
Past streets I grew up on
past duck ponds and tree clumps
hens warming their egg batch
wet silage and dry hay.
Past flies buzzing the dung steam
horses snorting the morning.
The distant haze of city
is a mirage of castles.

Now a sparrow lying in the tracks
wrapped in its wings
fish swimming on their sides
in rivers of raw sewage
and my train
roaring past alleys of lost cats
brick dust and chimney soot,
roaring past fallen window washers
men with hearts and dragons on their arms
and women with iron wedding rings --
all accustomed to inglorious death,
each one there for an instant
alive and suddenly gone.

There is a chaos of switches
a bridge and its rumble
an absence of sun
and slowly. . .slowly. . .stop.
I go off to pay homage to the clock
where the eye squints and the skin dries
while my train waits
lying fallow in diesel huff --
waiting to take me home.

EXECUTIVE MATERIAL

He is always dictating letters
adding up his serious numbers.
She is always typing fast
her hair as black as typewriter ribbon --
the two of them formal and polite.

On weekends he is a rider of horses.
The tub in his bathroom has lion's feet.
His living room chairs have lion's feet.
His dining room table has lion's feet.
When he dreams of himself
he is always on horseback.

Once he looked into her eyes. . .
amber flowers breathing summer
small ponds flecked with colored snails.
He turned away and shuffled his papers.
Once he looked into her eyes. . .
twin gulls. . .
twin hopes. . .
small bright cages of sunlight.
He added up his serious numbers.

Once she looked into his eyes. . .
home movie memories. . .empty rooms.
Once she looked into his eyes. . .
his wall became a screen
became a mask
became a glaze.
Pitiful part-time rider of horses.
Paltry man of lion's feet.

He will always be dictating letters
adding up his serious numbers
dreaming of himself as always on horseback.
She will always be typing fast,
no longer looking into his eyes,
her hair like a fading typewriter ribbon.

ON THE ROAD FROM HERE TO THERE

In the wilds of Nebraska where the flaming moon
turns to silver the fields of stubble,
where car lights grope from sign to sign
that tell the distances to Somewhere Else
there is a restaurant I could never find again.
Beer and hot dogs. Beer and fish.
Rivers and barrels and ponds of coffee --
enough to percolate the ceiling brown.

The talking and smoking, the need to be heard
above the dishes' clatter and the juke box bang.
An elk's head on the wall.
pictures of proud fishermen with their fish
and everyone talking. . .everyone talking.
And the princess of all women --
half schoolgirl, half bawd --
swaying her tray as she leaves for the kitchen,
her absence like the space between dreams
the death between lives.
Each swing of the kitchen door
a quick glimpse of ladies and knives, ·
pots and kettles and bright-colored bowls --
like anatomy, or the workings of a clock.

A man speaks of dinosaurs and prehistoric times.
In some village of Poland everyone wears his face.
        "They've just made another find --
        bunch of bones ten miles from here --
        big old things used to klump around.
        Crush you like an egg."
A madonna of cigarettes and wine,
a baby on her smiling knees
sits warm and safe from the endless fields
where monsters used to roam.

        "Then one day they all disappeared -- Poof!
        No one knows what happened. Just gone! Gone!"

"What? You believe that stuff?
Nothing just disappears. Got to be a reason."

One by one they leave --
out to the night of stubble and stars
and blind trees feeling the prairie air --
leave the beer and coffee and smoke
and well-built wonderful womanhood waitress
to start their engines and drive away
from the restaurant I never could find again.

LYING ON THE GROUND

Clouds with faces keep shifting about
and maple trees take root in the sky.
The honkings of duck trains hang in the air
to mingle with cries of squad cars in heat.

But under the grass lies another world --
cables roaring their buried secrets
over and over and all at once
of "Meet me down by the boat house tonight"
or "Ben, you hardly ever call"
-- man voice of chest hair and day-old beard,
smooth-skinned woman voice fading away.

And there's the turbulent rush of pipes
moving the lake from there to here
and the giant drains sucking and tumbling,
sloshing the endless sewage away.
Like resting my head on an animal's belly
listening to trickling waves of sound --
worms plastering their tunnels with slime
as they drill matrix paths around the world,
tree roots and rose roots feeling for life,
iris and jonquil bulbs swelling and pressing
deep in their darkness of slow birth.

I hear decomposing cats and dogs
once loved and living and purring and barking
in the surrounding houses. Or the sound of moles,
of gophers and subterranean grubs.
And buried weapons -- ticking bombs,
rusting revolvers and bladeless knives --
bullets lodged in collapsed skulls,
hair and nails growing and growing
as rivers of pain drain into the soil
down, down to the underground ocean,
souls locked up in caverns of clay,
weeping like sacred statues.

A giant magnet is the earth,
drawing down everything that lives --
leaves and trees and ships and birds.
A giant recycling machine,
giver of life and life's destroyer.
But I've had enough of lying here.
I should leave or I'll blend with cannons and cars
and pennies and rings and watches and wine,
should go to the crowded downtown streets
of pushing and shoving and laughing and swearing
where I'm supposed to be.

ICE FISHING

This is no place to be in winter,
its chain of grey days welded together
and the sky almost close enough to touch.
The birds are somehwere hiding in their feathers
and frogs are hibernating in their caves.
Even the spider webs are brittle from the cold.
I am the only sign of life
walking to the center of the lake,
its bleakness borrowed from the moon,
its foot of ice my substitute for faith.

I chop a hole this much by that
just large enough for fish I plan to catch
and sit there waiting, a part of winter.
They're down there, swimming through landscapes
of bottles and aging rocks,
swimming through wounds of sunken boats
knowing I'm up in their sky of ice
planning to whisk them off to heaven
or wherever it is they go.

But this winter. . .this cold.
Snow covers the husks of grasshoppers and ants
and bulbs lie lifeless in the iron earth.
Maybe I'll be found here half alive
or frozen like a duck to its pond,
a buoy bell desolately dinging in the wind
and a lung-full of breath like cotton candy
clinging to my lips.
And surrounding me those houses along the shore,
snow draped on their roofs like carpets,
all of them warm with fires and feather beds,
each with someone in the kitchen sipping tea,
each with its broiled fish lying on a platter
with almonds and onions and twists of lemon,
its fish-eyed eyes still wondering why.

I suppose some intellectual fish down there
is studying the lethal aspects of the hook,
trying to calculate the angle of approach
necessary for removal of the bail
without totally mangling his jaw
or puncturing his brain.
Even pondering if the prize is worth the risk.
But now such findings would be purely academic --
the hole has frozen solid and I'm going home.

SUCCESS

My third and final wish is, once again
to see that oldest of ancient movies --
half out of sync, half worn away
of Harley Klint or some actor no one knows
playing someone I somehow feel is me
whistling through the New York City spring
this song that just pops in his head.
Old time cars moving through the streets.
Birds happy. Dogs happy.
He steals an apple. Buys a rose.
Does the tango with a milkman's horse.

The song sticks in his head, he jots it down,
pecks at it on the piano in his room
then makes the rounds of music publishers --
short ones with baggy jowls
tall ones with turkey skin --
cigarette smoke, derby hats -- the works --
all screaming, "Out! You call that music?"
or "Give up, son. Sell life insurance.
Run away to sea."

Close-up of his shoes all worn and always walking,
his song played in a minor key to show exhaustion.
Then wandering in the magic music store
where sweet young girl piano player
dreams at him and plays his song for him,
he singing it to the curl of her hair
to the music of her face.
Cleaning women drop their mops and dance,
the owner of the store starts dancing
and people from the street come in and sing.
Faces of some who never smiled before
begin to crack at last.

The piano becomes a full-fledged orchestra.
Motorists are on their car roofs dancing.
And pedestrians dressed like Balkan peasants
begin to sing and kiss and dance
and street cleaners dance. . .school teachers dance. . .
the girl piano player's father's chauffeur dances.
Even kindly old cop tears up all his tickets.
Oh, it's enough to make your eyes water --
the world as it should be.

Shot of miles of music rolling from the presses,
of stacks of dollars piling high.
And there they are, young and in love and suddenly
he, by some strange miracle, dressed in a tuxedo
and this girl, all flouncy white and sequins
and every inch Miss Universe
waving from their open limousine,
moving through ticker-tape parades
to Happily Ever After. End of show.
Oh, what a a lovely world this is.
Tomorrow I think I'll try to write a song.

THE UNIVERSITY CLUB

Of course he must have been a member
though not the sort you'd care to know.
Obviously just some Felix Nobody --
large baldheaded man in wrinkled suit,
always near the window in the dining room
reading some book or other as he ate,
gazing down at traffic in the street
or listening to foghorns groaning in the harbor.

Every night he ordered octopus --
the only one, what's more, who ever did --
Octopus Flambeau with creole sauce and wine,
Octopus Del Monico or Octopus Kiev.
Or casserole, croquets, or chowder,
Voracious appetite for octopus.

Twice after they passed the rule allowing women
he brought the same disreputable floozy
who drank too much chablis, of course,
and prattled on in such a senseless way
with catfish gumbo oozing from her lips.
Her fingers twined like ivy around the glass,
her legs wound around his beneath the table
and she sang some strangely silly gurgling song
much to the embarrassment of everyone.

The head waiter was told to speak to him
if he should ever bring her there again.
But for months he ate alone --
Octopus Almondine. . .
Octopus a la King. . .
occasionally swimming up from the caverns of his book
to look down at the traffic or listening to the harbor,
often with tears welling in his eyes.

One evening she returned,
so common with her flimsy dress and dangling beads.
They laughed and drank their wine
and sang their song
as she brazenly wrapped his legs with hers.
But when the waiter finally approached their table,
bristling brows and iron jaw,
she made a little purple-inky cloud
and poof! They suddenly disappeared.

THE PARTY

"Keep your eyes on this watch.
See how it sparkles the light from the ceiling?"
I grow drowsy looking at it.
"Now I will count down from ten. Nine, eight.
When I reach one you will become invisible. . .
six, five, and return when I snap my fingers
and not remember a thing,
four, three. . ." Fred still counting.

But nothing happens -- everyone
politely wandering off to the kitchen or the porch.
Only Christine, sort of half gangly, half stately
with that smile that uses every line of her face,
but now no smile -- suddenly serious.
And Fred with his book on Hypnotism Self-Taught
smiling in spite of what I think is his failure.
I say, "Let's eat something, Christine,"
but she just looks around and then
walks through me to the bedroom for her coat.

"Hey, Fred! I can't see my hands!
Come on -- she walked right through me!
Snap your fingers, Fred. This is no joke."
But he's forgotten me, just sits
flashing his smile, flashing his white teeth
and finally goes home, me following, shouting,
"Fred! Fred! Snap your fingers!"
Even as he sleeps I shout
thinking he'll hear me in his dreams.
Even pound him, but my fists go through nothing.

I keep trying to kill Fred, but nothing works.
The rain falls through me
and dogs whimper when I come around.
The loneliest sort of wilderness,
but damned if I'll go around crying for help.
Still, what to do?
Walk some endless beach without leaving a track?
Sit on bar stools forgetting what thirst is?
Go snooping through walls?

I follow Fred around willing him to snap his fingers.
Crawl into his brain and command him, but he won't.
Do I have to be there when he snaps his fingers?
Do I have to hear the sound of it?
What if he snaps them while I'm in Christine's room
touching her face like dust on a moth's wing?
Or lying next to her watching her sleep?
"Someday, Fred, you'll snap your fingers by mistake
and then look out!
I'll get you, Fred."

QUIET ZONE

On streets where the earth shudders on its axis
and squad cars dash about like injured flies,
the windows are dark with sleep.
The serenades of ritual courtship.
an occasional cry for help from the alley,
high heels churning their way down the sidewalk
are all as much a part of night as stars.
Parties on the other side of the wall,
the bawdy sons of stein-clanking voices,
are lullabies that hang in the air.

But there is no sleep to be had in the country
with the sound of bulbs swelling in the earth
or the small river twisting in its bed.
The pulse of birds huddled under the eaves
or the pink breath of the old cow
kneeling in the manger, if that's what it is,
are a roar that kills all hope of sleep.
The huge trees who have never left home
rattle their leaves through the life-span of night
and now and then a guillotine down the hall
slams on the neck of some red-eyed mouse.
Perhaps before someone starts butchering cabbage
I can catch the early morning bus
back to my city of easy sleep.

REUNION OF THE THIRD PLATOON

They drink while half the stars set,
laugh and talk lightly
of life and death with the Third Platoon
their eyes bright with the ritual of telling
heroic and proud
but still very much like aging clerks.

Telling of Dietrick and Chavez and Henderson
running through the flaming village
drifting over the streets unaware of their legs.
How Maloney was pitchforked as soon as he landed --
staring up at the sky he had dropped from,
a small bubble of death on his lips.
Or Murphy, how he braced himself on a rock --
his machine gun barrel hot,
flies laying eggs in his wounded shoulder.

Now Anderson talking. Now Roberts --
his hands describing battles and barracks
but not the night he had DEATH BEFORE DISHONOR
tattooed on his arm --
half drunk on two beers
imagining medals on his first uniform
just fresh from the warehouse.

Never a word about Stein going mad
still keeping a pistol under his pillow
dreaming pantomine battles
the same bullet burning his gut over and over
or how Sergeant Bartoli grows sad and vague
if he sees a dead bird or a butterfly wing.
His wife says he sits too much alone.

No one mentions next year. . .or meeting again.
But they'll all be back
except maybe Peters, who seemed out of breath
several times tonight
or Williams, who always acts restless
when they get together like this.

FUGUE

In the land of the raised fist
the brandished rifle, the knife in the teeth
the screaming through streets of mosque and minaret
to keep alive the ancient hates
one man abandons for a day
the idiotic acts of history
and follows his neglected path
through narrow streets of donkeys and shops
to the silken rooms of his black-haired woman,
her eyes of camel and sand
of stars of flame in the dome of night
and speaks to her of a fertile oasis
as she draws the shade and shuts the door.

In the land of toppled statues and the iron rose,
of formations of bombers in the perfect sky,
of parades of ponderous bombs through the square,
through the closely guarded streets,
one man ignores for awhile
the stupid seriousness of history
and goes with longing in his eyes
through streets of laundry and Slavic steeples
through neighborhoods of onion-shaped roofs
to the dark varnished rooms of his heavy-thighed woman
her eyes of samovars and hardwood forests
of lake ice cracking in the spring
and speaks to her of stars on the Volga
as she draws the shade and shuts the door.

In the land of crowded subways and highway rush
of news of wars and soldiers somewhere else
and security under the missile-webbed skies
one man foresakes for a day
the frightening twists of history
and goes, as he's been wanting to,
through streets of traffic and flashing signs
through neighborhoods of fenced-in lawns
and house-broken dogs and secretive cats
to the tidy room of his cluttered woman,
her eyes of typewriters and drug store breakfasts
of dances danced and evenings alone
and speaks to her of a lake in Wisconsin
as she draws the shade and shuts the door.

THE VICTORS

Heat lies on the road in silver ponds
and sterile clouds turn yellow in the sky.
For three days, now, the battle on the plains
has been drawing closer --
guns crackling and faraway shouts,
and a faint decay that is part of the air.
Finally the remnants of Caudillo's men,
their faces lost in their beards,
come shuffling through the heat and dust
with not a horse remaining.
They pass the withered poplars that ring the palace,
barely a platoon of shredded uniforms
and clanking rifles and drinking cups.

Their prize is an empty building.
El Presidente and his family have fled.
And the ministers.
And all the guards.

They quietly smoke the best cigars,
gouge the mahogany desk with their boots,
drink up the brandy and wine.
They have built a fire on the marble floor,
scoop fish from the pool with their hats
and, like Christ at his picnic,
cook them all.

The patio has become a campsite --
Fire Fish and Lung Fish and Canchitos
all fried together.
Bright Jewel Fish and rare Silver Bark
skewered and roasted on the same stick.
Fish as transparent as air,
blue fish and copper fish, ebony and green,
sizzle in strips over the fire.
The conquerors of the palace,
plumes of color crammed in their mouths,
drool morsels of rainbow when they laugh.

And then, revived by food,
reassured by survival, they rest,
fall to the floor in a dull sleep
until, halfway through night but long before dawn
while the stars are setting one by one,
they leave their palace of fish heads and conquest
and wander back home to the hills.

THE RHINO CORRIDA

In a time and place where reason slept
there was pageantry and pomp
and the caged rhinoceros.
    Golden trumpets in the sun
    and three matadors pacing their perfect horses,
    each with his muleta and sword,
    red silk and flashing steel.
The cheering and color, the heat and the trumpets --
it was all part of the afternoon.

Six picadors rode Arabian horses
bright streamers tied to their javelins
silver braid on their three-cornered hats.
    On foot were the city officials
    the fiesta committee
    and a few civil servants and clerks.
The stadium was a constant roar --
roses in the air
roses in the arena
and everyone talking or waving.

A flourish of trumpets and the riders dismounted,
but this time the crowd was quiet.
Cigar smoke and felt hats.
Noblemen's wives with their white mantillas.
    When the gate of the cage was raised
    there was a sign like the wind in the wheat.
    The rhinoceros ran across the arena.
    His sides and neck were steel plate,
    his eyes in an iron mask.
Two birds the color of mud
flew from his shoulders.

Oh the rage of the rhinoceros
and the power of his horn.
    There were cheers from the valiant matadors
    flicking their red muletas
    standing poised with swords
    and for the bravery of the picadors
    blunting javelin on the castiron beast.
But then the cries of disbelief
at the goring of the horses,
at the crackle of bone
as heads were flattened in the sand.
And the screams as the rhinoceros
tore through the stands, making a mulch
of soldiers and gamblers and lovers
and pregnant women and boys in sailor suits.

The following days were days of mourning.
But how useless grief is
when reason has been sleeping.
Tears lose all their meaning.
Even the church bells make a foolish sound.

WORLD WAR FOUR

How unsuspecting the Asiatics are.
And at such a complete loss to understand
why they keep shrinking in size
why their curbstones seem higher every day
and their stairs more difficult to climb.
They are constantly shortening the legs
of their tables and chairs.

Based on reports from our High Command
We should conquer their continent in a matter of months
now that we have perfected our Regressive Genetic Ray
and are beaming it down from unseen satellites.

Meanwhile the enemy grows smaller and smaller.
Last week when the president of Hyderabad
gave his emergency message from the palace balcony
to the little crowd jammed in the square
he had to stand on a packing crate
to be seen over the railing.
And an estimated one hundred soldiers
of the Northeast Federated Provinces
were lost when snow slid from their barracks roof.

Soon, when the time is right. . .when they are too small
to lift their guns or fly their planes
we will invade --
send in some nurses and corpsmen
who will ship them all, like so many dolls, to Sri Lanka,
that pearl of the Indian Ocean whose soil and climate
can easily support such a vast little population.
This type of warfare, we contend,
is a major breakthrough for humanitarian ethics.

But disconcerting reports are reaching us from Canada --
motorists no longer fitting in their cars
and people having to be cut from their houses.
Travelers tell of a nation of giants,
stressing that this change has been rather sudden.
Our relations with Canada have always been friendly,
but an army of Paul Bunyans poses an obvious threat.
They could easily cross the border
and trample our military like so many grapes.

Undoubtedly these are very troubled times.

ISADORA DUNCAN

Born broke in the San Francisco hills
thirty years after the lust for gold,
out of the cradle endlessly dancing
to ocean waves and random winds
running and bending and pausing and floating
to streams of music that flow forever,
to delicatessens and butcher shops --
flute lyre and horn and harp,
Chopin, Mozart and Satie,
dancing the course her life is to take --
up and up and down and down --
bright waves on fathomless water.

Cloven-hoofed piper drawing her on
to rickety stages and music halls
and doddering cattle boat to London.
Dance without music. . .Dance without shoes. . .
Berlin, Vienna and Budapest
suddenly merging from girl to woman --
white tunic and golden sandals,
showers of sunlight and lilies on water,
scenery of Greek and Egyptian temples
and endless cries of "Isadora!"
as young men of the audience
remove the horses from her carriage
and pull her, sing to her through the streets.

From a chronically love-sick begetter of children
receiving a daughter --
form and movement. . .emotion as force. . .
tambourines and jangling bells.
From a kindly old millionaire, a son --
always dance upward. . .never dance down. . .
pipes and drums and concertinas
raging through the blood.

The children! The children! The beautiful children!
They with their little leapings and runnings
until the automobile they're in
rolls backward into the River Seine --
drowned like kittens in a sack.

After that the bad days come dancing
tumbling and clattering over each other
and all the hours and days and years
with their sorrows of regret drift by
until dance becomes religion,
her school for little girl dancers the church. . .
Sibelius and Mendelssohn. . .Bartok and Bach. . .
she, the priestess, floats through the air
with all the neophyte Isadorables
hopping and leaping behind her.

Her school for dancing children in Moscow,
the gracefulness of her marble body
motion springing from emotion
until she marries a Russian poet
just for the music of his words --
little pancake and caviar man
who follows her halfway around the world
with all his absurdity and tears --
writes his last poem with blood from his wrists
and hangs himself in the hotel closet

while Isadora. . .Isadora
dancing with veils or without,
dances her way to the French Riviera
where her scarf makes love to a racing car's wheel
and ends her dancing forever.

SUBJECT MATTER

All these stacks of grassy pools and cut flowers
and fruit on the table, and fish. . .
Sometime I'd like to paint Juanita,
her frightened eyes. . .her calm, classic eyes. . .
oil on canvas, or maybe acrylic.
Maybe wearing a bracelet or rings,
but nothing else -- just her.
Maybe holding a cluster of grapes. . .or a glass,
her head tossed back -- big bacchanalian scene
with cloven-hoofed piper in the background
or old pot-bellied lush with grapes for a beard
ogling her with drunken fascination.

Or maybe some desolate, almost midnight backdrop,
everything floating about in the eye of a storm
or a Witches' Sabbath on top of Bald Mountain --
hawks with serpents in their beaks,
leafless trees reaching out to her
and she wearing a crown of precious stones.
Maybe add some white for contrast --
a lamb in its meadow, or a long-haired cat.

But Juanita wouldn't do it. Much too skittish.
More apt to slip some tasteful picture of herself
under the door, expecting me to work from that --
hazy September Morn sort of thing
of her with a dozen flying scarves
or wearing a pristine little tutu
left over from some high school dance recital.

Or worse -- show up with her sad-faced family
there to protect their closely guarded daughter --
big pillowy mother, scraggly migrant father
and little brothers whining in their native tongue,
all standing like they just got off the boat
while I try to recapture the groove of her upper lip,
the way her earlobes fasten above the neck,
or painting out the moss beneath her arms
and covering those first bold plans
with veils and leotards.

Maybe Mrs. Kraus would be a better model,
she with those ex-lovers floating face-down in her heart,
though she's sprung her supple lines with beer and cabbage
and cracks her knuckles when there's nothing else to do.
I see her topless with blue skirt and Phrygian cap
defending the barricades of Paris
or even something more teutonic --
possibly with helmet, breast plates and a sword
as her Valkyrie friends ride through the sky,
though who could paint the housewife out of her?
Maybe still life would be better after all --
an apple lying on the table.
Or maybe a dead fish.

LE GRAND NU BLEU

On this, the third day of creation
all is quiet in the life class studio
with Rita Flannery almost fully cloned
on a dozen canvases in progress,
still standing, bending like a harp
as the students paint her in her various ways.

One sees her with angora cats and vines and doves,
another as Botticelli's Venus born full-blown
standing in the golden half shell,
her auburn hair unfurled in the non-wind.

Here she's shown with little voyeur men
and business men and shallow, sallow pallid men
and would-be lovers sad with hunger,
all memorizing torso curves of hip and thigh,
of neck through arm to wrist to hand,
the gentle slope to mysteries of planetary breasts
and areola rose windows of miniature cathedrals.

One has her bathing on a golden balcony
of dieffenbachia and parakeets and monkeys,
one with cloudbursts over raging mountain streams
and one with hanging gardens, trumpets and guitars.

Then finally, at a certain time,
the paints are put away, the brushes cleaned,
the canvases are filed in racks to dry
and each painter leaves, wanting to be Pygmalión,
to have his painting come alive for him to love.
And Rita Flannery, covered by a blanket,
steps down from the tub, dresses and goes home
fading in the rush hour subway crunch
disguised with shopping bag and winter coat.

ON LIVING TOO CLOSE TO THE MUSIC SCHOOL

The sound-drenched neighbors rock on their porches.
Their heads sway like daffy metronomes
and their hands trace rhythms in the air.
How can the birds sleep under the eaves
or settle down in their steel wool nests?

What migrant souls these students have
that escape from their studios by saxophone
and set the sky on fire
or lace guitar chords through the trees
on their journey to the stars or through the window.

Nights of twig-snap and frog-song cushion in my sleep --
even truck rumble or dog howl
or an occasional distant shot,
but not a girl who sings to me in flute sounds
nor the jealous piano that warns me in dominant fifths.

But how can I disregard her
when she calls to me through the walls
on nights when the moon lies pouched in marsupial clouds
and tells me she's watching me from the cosmos,
tells me her hair is draped over the river,
tells me by flute that she's slowly becoming a tree?

I'll leave.
I'll move away,
but not while that violent piano is there.
If I show the least indication of fear
it will follow me wherever I go
and some day attack me with sharp staccatos
and leave me lying dead in the street.

THE RED SHOES

I've seen the movie so many times --
now I'm even writing about this girl, this Moira,
her walk more of a skip than a walk
out where the leaves blow or the lake roars
or lambs nibble the stubbled grass.
Half-notes and quarter-notes slip from her lips
as she hums her contentment.
Even jammed in a crowd that is more like a river
she stands out by her red hair bouncing.
Even in the office where she types
she walks as though seagulls are in the air
and she barefoot on the shore.

But what ominous portent sort of day is this?
She wanders by a shoe store on Van Buren Street
where swarthy little Italian cobbler elf,
his voice the strum of a faint guitar,
stands like the shadow of the bird
reaching out from his tomb of a shop
proffering, offering her these shoes. The Red Shoes
that drive whoever wears them mad with dancing.
He says, "You like?" Then Poof! They're on her feet
and he, with smoke and flame behind his eyes
hops about like a cricket or some crazy bug.

Suddenly a woman, then a priest
reach out to hold her back, clutch at her gauzy skirt.
But The Red Shoes force her to dance
through streets of frantic piano and erotic flute
past blue houses with cats in their windows,
anonymous houses with hollow cheeks.
She dances to her room with its stuffed dog
and souvenir pillows and covered bird cage,
dances through her office that has turned to jade
with emerald desks and floors of gold,
through streets of tolling bells

where her lover stares at her with icicles for eyes,
dances through the decapitated night,
through the rain and off to the bright stars.

The neighbors watch her from their voyeur window.
At dawn her dress reflects the sun.
Clouds drift from their puddles
and drops no longer drip from the eaves.
She dances with newspapers in the streets
as the piano becomes a languid saxophone.

Now things grow hazy. Was it a train
that struck her? Or a truck? Maybe fatigue.
The people standing near wear noncommittal masks
and watch her lying crumpled on the ground,
a string of pearls around her throbbing throat.
She dies in the movie, but I am writing this.
I decide, No -- she will live, and tenderly remove
The Red Shoes from her feet. The crowd smiles.
Flowers bloom in the windows above us.
I take her hand and we walk off together.
I still haven't decided where.

NICK FUENTES

Not about him -- about his horn, his trumpet --
no longer shiny, almost polished gold,
but battered now from bouncing down the cliff
and left to lie there by the trickling river.
Like King Arthur's sword, like the bowl of Ulysses,
a trumpet only he could play --
he, Nick, of the heavy red face and thick black hair.

No longer a trumpet full of roses,
a flaming trumpet in the sky
that would make your eyes moist if you heard it,
that would turn the desert bright with flowers,
turn the clouds to chocolate, the sky to yellow straw,
make the old turkey-neck men on the porch steps
feel young and smile their gold-toothed smiles.
Oh the sound of it -- down to the roots of your hair
to the very fundament of your guts,
make you want to rub your face with its sound
rub your very flesh
make every leaf of the tree pray never to fall.

Then why, in La Droma Tavern
did they jump on his trumpet, throw it down the cliff
bouncing from rock to rock to destruction
then punch Nick's lips against his teeth
so he could never play again,
toss him after it not caring if he died?
Maybe the Indian blood. . .maybe the Spanish.
But that music, it tore at them, reviving their madness
brought them face to face with their vanished childhood
with their dead parents, with all the dead loves
they were straining to forget.
Brought back forgotten sorrows, forgotten faces,
rainy afternoons of steeples holding up the sky.
Made them almost want to love again.
Made them scream their contagious quarrels.
Made them face their forgotten selves.

They should have let him go. Now all they hear
is his trumpet, the anguish of each note
like a haze that hangs over the mountain,
like an endless rain, like the memory of special moons.
It is everywhere -- in the mud streets
in the paintless shacks of the sad-faced families
in the winding streets of the lonely town,
the loveless town. It gnaws at them,
slashes them, enters the rooms of the young girls
who lie in their beds like voluptuous stones
and invades the perimeters of their sleep,
winds through the halls like wisteria vines
as the hard faces, the soft faces,
live like the trickling river. . .
as the waxing, waning moon
shines down on the battered trumpet.

OPTIONS

The ballerinas have grown heavy
about the thigh and in the eye,
twirl slower, leap a little lower every year
evolving weightless gliding to a thump.
So is it any wonder that they ponder
other ways of paying for and tasting
this sweet Dolce Vita life?

Of course it's all too soon to contemplate surrender --
joining the birdsie little ladies with their
lavender dry armpit lives, or drinking
with the landlord in his room where nothing grows
or rehearsing the sweet and strong endearing
wifey look -- escaping into marriage
discovering the frog remains a frog
and not a prince in spite of all the kisses,
discovering so dramatically it's either
a dagger in the lung or this dwelling in froggy bliss
in his castle of poor taste,
enduring rituals of walking hand in hand each evening
to the bench by the tree on the street where
the bridge crosses the river and the boat floats down
on time, each time tooting its little whistle.

And then hand in hand in darkness, returning
to lie in bed, sometimes talking, sometimes not
and finally dreaming of sailing through the air
all white and filmy flimsy, drifting out of the arms
of Baryshnikov and back again, over and over and over
until one night of pterodactyl scream,
one night of birds with serpents in their beaks
when one of them seeps up through the ceiling
leaving a frog husk or a dancer husk lying there in bed
with the usual expression of togetherness content.

But after all, what does one do?
Certainly not wait while clocks of the sleeping town
cancel out the moon's pull
nor be the aging Salome, dancing forever,
wearing a brassiere the size of two men's hats
nor standing waiting for someone cursed with glands
that make him roam the streets.

Better to lie singing on the rocks, waiting for some
semi-functional Ulysses lashed to the mast of his ship
and stroll with him through enchanted landscapes
or statues and amphora on the ocean floor.

MISS GREEN

Be not dismayed, Old Maid,
that the Invisible Man hides in your room
or is playing kneesies with you on the bus.
Why he could have any dreamy little
gooey little harlequin romantic,
silver in the eyelids, dimpled in the cheek,
his voice speaking softly in her ear,
his voice like the whisper of wheat
or small birds of a distant mountain.

Besides, it's Miss Green he's after,
Miss Green of whom he dreams invisible dreams
as he waits for her through the dark-star night
as she lies sleeping. It must be he
who's been breathing at her door
and tapping his fingers on her roof.
And on that evening of swamps gone wild
with frog delight, who but he, the Invisible Man
goaded by compulsions to create, could have
slipped through the window and down the hall
to the room where she slept her fastidious sleep?
She, so always primly correct and executive sweet
was on that night playing the role of garden
for his invisible begetting.

Oh, Miss Green, so always in command of herself
but suddenly toppled --
so respected, but now so gradually laughed at,
burgeoning great with invisible child
and reduced to studying hazy phases of the moon,
waiting in seclusion under her Dieffenbachia
for her time of invisible fulfillment.
And for, of all things, an invisible son,
the image of his father -- labelled "false"
by obstetricians and other puzzled doctors
who'd never seen a thing they couldn't see.

And what's worse, she learned nothing from it all
except to bolt her door at night and lie in bed
studying the mechanical planets through her window.
Occasionally she hears a sigh in the chimney,
a whisper at the door,
a wind that makes gaps between the windows cry,
"I want him! Where's my son?"

DEAR OLD GALL BLADDER, FAREWELL

I'm really in no frame of mind for this --
counting down from ninety-nine and all.
Besides, what if I don't make it?
What if the oscillometer stops beeping
and I rise drifting to the snow white ceiling
looking down while they give shocks to the old husk
or pound the ribs trying to bring me back
so I can pay the bill.

And what if I never live again? Will I be reduced
to popping up from time to time tediously
spelling out messages on dusty ouija boards
whenever someone has nothing else to do?
Or maybe even have some spooky medium summon me
to her darkened dining room to put on my act
for the gathering of apprehensive ladies there.
What if the Chinese have the real answer --
that I'll join my ancestors? Will I be forced to listen
to Granddad relive the Battle of Bull Run
or Uncle Walter tell his rotten jokes forever?

Maybe I'll stand in line up to my knees in dry-ice vapors
waiting my turn with billions of other luckless souls
who enjoyed being invisible for a day or so
but find that life's no fun without a body to inhabit.
And what sort of lottery will it be?
What if I become some savage spending my entire life
naked as a plucked duck in some undiscovered jungle
picking my teeth after eating raw kuala bear?
Or worse -- an Eskimo, needing at least three squaws
to wrap around me through the six-month night.
Or maybe a Bedouin wrapped in sheets
constantly racing across the burning sands,
waving a rifle from Ain-Salah to Fez
and sleeping at night with some halitosis camel.

But what if there's no planet left to put me on
just when I need it most, the whole place pulverized away
by those unbendable folks with their castiron governments?
Does that mean floating about in limbo all through time
without a robe or dog or slippers or warm bed
or even a sunrise to wake up to every morning?

What comes after eighty? Sixty-eight or fifty-nine?
Hey, Doc -- I've got a hunch you'd like this.
Give yourself a jab and come along.

SANCTUARY

The world has smelly feet.
The world has fleas.
Maybe I should take some name like Fra Belevolent,
buy a dark robe and join some working order monastery
its chapel a castle, its grounds with wooded paths
where, every dawn, sad-eyed monastics
wander past flowers and statues of angels,
each reading his little Latin psalter
and mumbling cryptic things.

Maybe I could work in the garden, be in charge of
thinning out carrots or hoeing rows of cabbage
and late each afternoon, when the sun is round and rosy
klump my sack of vegetables on the zinc-topped table
for the steamy-faced little buxom nun to slice and clean,
she with hair strands stuck to her forehead,
smiling, blushing up at me as I cautiously study
the delightful contours of her habit
aching to tweak her slightly here and there.

Maybe spend my time cloistered away praying too much,
the moon spreading its silver on the roof,
even shining through to touch me with its madness --
praying until I grow ephemeral and levitate,
sail above the trees amazing everyone. Or in the spring
watch measly little birds that can't fly yet,
their parents up above the chirping cat warnings.
They'd come to me for peace and refuge
until at last I'm St. Benevolent of the Birds.

Maybe I was born to ring the chapel bells,
pull down on the rope with all my weight and then
be yanked back in the air with each resounding ictus,
the overtones of it shattering through my blood.
But I suppose, in time, some Brother Holier-Than-Thou
would want to ring, demand to ring, the bells --
he who was almost blinded travelling to Damascus --
so what sort of chance would that leave me?

And if I were far behind the rest in miracles,
couldn't make a bush burn or make snakes from sticks,
I'd wind up scrubbing floors or giant pots and pans.
Pathetic ending. I'll just skip the monastery act
and put up with this world a little longer.

NATHAN

Loretta,
married to the house she was born in,
washing its windows, scrubbing its floors,
polishing silver to please her mother
who floats above her near the ceiling
and Father, gone to Hell of course.
The souvenir spoons, the teacup collection,
the dinky doilies on the sofa
wrinkled as the house is wrinkled,
as the corners of her eyes
as the edges of her voice.

Old chairs that no one may sit on,
especially the tedious, straight-backed men
who have no odor in their clothes --
secretive eyes and well-tended nails,
teacups balanced on their knees --
some lost in the desert of their books
with mirages of topless library ladies,
some lost in silence, turning to marble
as flowers in their vases bloom and wilt,
as Loretta sits like a hole in space
her beads rolling up and down with her breathing --
never a thought of paths not taken
or regretting unheld conversations.

But Nathan, tracking mud on the floor,
leaning the grease of his hair on the wall,
speaking of girl-fights and tavern brawls
and skinny-dipping in the lake --
Neptune in his third house,
Leo with Aquarius rising.
Gravy on the tablecloth,
bacon on the windowshades,
Loretta's anger driving him out.

At night in the shadowy living room
the plants strain to stay alive.
Under the drunk primavera moon
the house shakes its rafters with laughter at her.
Loretta, asleep in the bed she was born in,
dreams her restless, recurring dream
of "Oh, my teacup! Oh, my chair!
Oh, my doily on the couch!"
but of all the men who had come to call,
remembering only Nathan.

THE ROYAL BARGE

Cleopatra on her Ship of Death
floats past the crowds that line the Nile --
blue sails and amber hull,
ivory and onyx inlaid in the mast
jasper, amethyst and jade,
and under a golden canopy
the young queen lounging on silken pillows
looking almost the same as always --
but her heart in a jar
her mouth of love-words turned to stone
and above her breasts a faint blotch
where the asp injected its twin fangs.

Her gown so rich and death so new
she seems alive, as though asleep,
as though she might wave as she often has
to all the two-dimensional people --
the almond-eyed women, the thin-legged children,
the warriors forgetting their swords and spears --
everyone crying out their grief,
their voices mixed with the raucous sounds
of horn and lyre and drum and flute
on that blue-sky and amber-sand afternoon.

Egypt, its phantoms of blood desires,
its serious reverence for shadows,
trapped in a patch of slowed-down time
under the hierglyphic clouds.
Boats transparent in the haze --
sampans from the Yellow Sea,
caiques from the isles of Greece --
all with their sails slack with mourning,
gulls soaring quietly over their masts.

The barge floating up the Nile,
at its tiller the handsomest of men
so honored by making this voyage of death,
slowly drifting beyond the city, beyond the towns
passing snakes asleep on their rocks
and frogs leaping from the shore,
passing the boundaries of late afternoon,
date palms and pelicans
rustling papyrus and ivory temples,
storks and stone lions with outspread wings.

Finally approaching the cosmic dark
of night birds lost in their bird sleep
and owls inscrutable in their trees
as the stars guide the ghostly barge,
as the moon spreads out its path on the water
and torches surrounding Cleopatra
merge with the sea's horizon.

A TALE OF TWO CITIES

Ronald Coleman,
all his life debauched and aimless,
stands clear-eyed and heroic
bound for the guillotine
in this, his finest hour.

White shirt open at the throat
he comforts the frightened, trusting blonde
as they ride together in the rocking tumbrel
through screaming streets of sewer stink
and raw tobacco spittle,
inching past the legless beggar
past the old vindictive bitch who watches
shaking her woman-ruins with loony laughter.
Then, from that carnival of popcorn, hamburgers and beer
comes the jeering and cries of the cloven-hoofed crowd
demanding his head on a platter
demanding tomato blood and giblet soup
screaming for the surprising yellow root of his being.

It is there in the sweet iambics of the afternoon
that Ronald Coleman, unbuttoner of dresses,
loosener of tresses,
dreamer. . .drinker of burgungy. . .
ascends the platform steps.
The guillotine is a shadow of its timbers.
And the lethal blade,
the basket for the noble heads,
the authorities so be-business-suited stern.
Even the executioner a man of hat, cravat and gloves
while Ronald Coleman, doomed but human,
looks up at the tumbling cotton clouds
looks down at the cobblestone people
looks far off at the rubber hills
beyond the fields of yesterday.

And it's then, in this best of times
in this worst of times
that he acts out his paltry destiny
of choosing death to marriage,
rambling on like some converted drunk
about this is the best thing he has ever done,
kneeling at last before the preposterous guillotine
that breaks him down to basic chemicals
and frees him from the tumult of his mind
while gradually a choir of sound-track voices
blends him with the breeze.

CLARK STREET BRIDGE

Why did Harvey
already partly dead with one bad eye
and several plastic teeth
choose this, the brightest of days,
to climb the railing of the Clark Street bridge
and so dramatically slide down,
down through the air and into the gangrene river?

And why did those men with their easily forgotten faces
stand watching as though it really didn't matter?
Why did all the discarded business men
lost in the sequence of their hazy days
sit playinng their impotent checkers,
their idiotic dominoes? And the women. . .
why did the women with their plunging necklines
keep glaring their equality, daring you to look?
And why did the vines keep eating trees?
Why did the cats keep eating birds?
Why couldn't someone have cried out,
"Stop him! Harvey. . .Don't!"

Maybe he was dying ever so slowly
in his syrupy remorse for paths not taken --
for never having married Sally fat and jolly
with whom only he could dance-two-three-kick
missing, thereby, living with her in heaven
over some grocery store with two, or who knows,
three grubby Sally children loving him,
climbing him like he was Gulliver
willing, if it came to that,
to sizzle on the funeral pyre with him.

Or friends. . .what if he'd lost his friends?
He, always so prone to hide behind his eyes
and speak so nervously of news and weather. . .
allergic to touch. . .cringing from hello's. . .

disguising himself with platitudes
to drive his friends away
but needing them. . .needing them.
Now and then mentioning uncomfortable things --
nostalgia for long-forgotten summers. . .
soft tar streets. . .cicadas sawing in the trees
or saying "roofs shingled with pigeons."
Saying ". .conjugations of the moon."

Why did the watchers watch, wearing their long
El Greco faces even as the final bubbles
bubbled up from where he fell?
Why couldn't a band of friends he never knew he had
have crooned to the river some gentle choral chorus,
hummed some Harvey requiem in voices like
paper sailboats sailing across the water
until he finally rose again, his flesh gone gray
with death. . .until he rose and let them lift him up
and carry him through the old familiar streets
and far away?

INSOUCIANCE

If the craven crow and the fierce-eyed hawk
     Swoop over the plain of my waste years
And the bright plans dwindle to fancy talk
     And hope is restrained by a thousand fears,
Mrs. Brady would dash up the walk waving recipes
for fried crow and hawk stew and ask me to speak
at her Woman's Club luncheon.

If Life throws up on my outstretched hand
     And Fate kicks the buttocks of my dreams
And my heart becomes a desert land
     Strewn with the bones of famished schemes,
Mrs. Brady would remark that there is so much of
that intestinal flu going around these days and
spend all afternoon showing me how bone chips can
make a delightful center-piece.

If the sun fades out in the black soot sky
     And the reaper comes, as he surely must,
Death-shroud draped over empty eye,
     Reducing endless time to dust,
Mrs. Brady would haggle with him a while and
finally agree to pay two dollars for the job
provided he doesn't forget that patch of grass
behind the garage and is sure to trim along the walk.

AT THE GRAVE OF MAXWELL BODENHEIM

He isn't there.
We've dug eight feet down with spades and trowels
pouring all the dirt through grading screens
and gathering up fragments large enough to hold
to be brushed off and studied later
but no Bodenheim --
only rusty bolts and bottle caps
nails and shards of coffee cups
and bits of what we thought were bone
but proved to be some sort of antler.

Perhaps he'd had enough of earth
feeling Death at his heels as he moved through
the skidrows of his world, and all the while
his head boiling with words and their echoes --
Beloved meaning woman meaning touch meaning warm,
Love meaning life with its pulse throb. . .
Since ascension has been proven possible
perhaps he's gone, one of the sleeping silver birds
nesting in Death's frozen hair.

So go on -- pay your respects.
Stand with your head bowed on the gravel path
along the grass where he's supposed to be.
Bring your flowers and stand with all those poets
who've made their pilgrimmage.
But don't believe the inscription
on that rain-smoothed rock.
"Here lies" is a lie.
There are no bones of Bodenheim resting here.

ROSEHILL

No one steals apples from the cemetery
where the pink euphoria bloom,
where stones that say Murphy or McGuire
are twined with nightshade, Columbine, and death.

What's more, no one wants to go there
except Al who now and then takes Ruth
and talks to her in spooky echo tones
until she hugs him out of fear,
or George who fondles the marble statues,
especially the wistful nymphs and angels
who stand topless in their stone robes.
And on sunny Sunday afternoon
the old big-bottomed women go there
placing flowers on Horace or Rebecca
who've been dead these many years.

But no one really wants to go there
except old What's-his-name on Chestnut street,
his eyes amber with cigarettes
his blood gone brown with coffee
hawking up death and his fingers yellow
and even he yearning for God's Blue Mountain,
not just some box beneath the poison apple tree.

And Miss Quinn with her cool oasis body
living at the Evanshire -- she's halfway there already,
clacking her knitting needles while her
outstretched cat sleeps off its all-night orgy.
But she doesn't count because she doesn't care --
been to all the tea-leaf readers
and knows about the Long Voyage Home
and years ago gave up her grottos and meditation
praying for some plot to her life,
praying to be taken to some old hotel,

slipping past the father of all night clerks
saying her name is Jones.
Oh Miss Quinn. . .Miss Quinn. . .
will her last-heard sound be the screech of brakes?
Or a shot?
Or gagging on nightmares in the Evanshire?

But it's all in the mind, that apple tree,
and there's no long-haired, dark-haired woman
sitting under the hanging moss of it
strumming her dulcimer,
and those apples are probably just like any other --
Winesaps, Jonathons, or McIntosh.
So go ahead -- try one and see.

MISS KATE

O Miss Kate, Miss Touch-me-not Miss Kate
so aloof in her carriage, so dry in the eye
so outraged by the grass-stained lovers
and made indignant by the moon
sits on the train with her carved face
thinking hot breath on her neck's nape
thinking fingers like hundreds of little mice
feeling her business suit.
Returns a glance by tugging her skirt
the imperceptible inch.

      Have you felt the rock's face
      Miss Kate, or the tree's bark?
      Have you felt the arm of the grocery boy
      or the moth's wing, have you
      felt the moth's wing or the bird's throat,
      felt the miracle of rabbit ears?

And as she sleeps, even as she sleeps
her up-tight hair prim on the pillow
her business suit sitting stern in the chair
Miss Kate dreams hands, dreams fingers, dreams
tongues that leave trails on her sancrosanct shoulders
dreams sweat of nutmeg, lips of brine
and faces on the subway train,
each one a path she might have taken,
dreams she's the disappearing woman
dreams jackpines swaying in the moonlight
dreams kissing her ceramic frog
until finally her hair lies loose on the pillow
her business suit flops limp in the chair
and car lights fondle the walls of her room.

THE TUNNEL OF LOVE

The carousel was horseless
and all the sounds of carnival were gone.
Still, up to the end of that last day
even while crowbars pried the
House of Mirrors down, the Greek
collected tickets for the Love Boat rides
sending us floating over and over
through arches of paint-flecked hearts
and bare-assed cherubs
into the cavern of the ancient shed
its water thick with oil and mud
its air the smell of wood rot
its sounds of girl-scream
hollow bump of boats
and treble twitter of precocious rats.

I think she had brown hair
had eyelids painted green
had beauty conjured by the power of the moon.
The two of us sat in the leaky skiff
pressed together. . .hands for eyes. . .
our feet dampened by the bilge
drifting on our slow and serious voyage
through total dark.

But why relive those Rubaiyat times?
The girl has disappeared into herself
is spawning reproductions of her husband
and the amusement park is gone
has, by some old wizard's spell,
become a shopping mall
with benches, fountains, and a shady walk
to hide its tumult.
And, except for always floating
back and forth from light to shadow
even I have changed.

THE PINES

How could I have known
on that December speck
of my mind's dark well
that the touch of lips in the frosty air
would cling like a hand to a frozen pump
through the spun-out years
of my long remembering?

How could I have known
on that day lost now
in the fuzz of time
when the wind-whipped waves of the eye blue lake
blotted out tracks in the sun warm sand
that the walk we walked would last this long
without a footprint showing?

How could I have known
on that warm-washed day
of a time-drowned year
when the wind blew words through the two tall pines
that we'd be sustained in that same green way,
and that those who listened to the wind
could hear the words between us?